St

Written by Dot Meharry
Illustrated by Trevor Pye

Stella is our new dog, but Stella doesn't listen.

We say, "Sit!"
but Stella doesn't sit.
She jumps.

We say, "Heel!"
but Stella doesn't
walk next to us.
She just rolls over.

We say, "Stay!"
but Stella doesn't stay.
She runs away.

We say, "Quiet!"
but Stella barks
and barks.

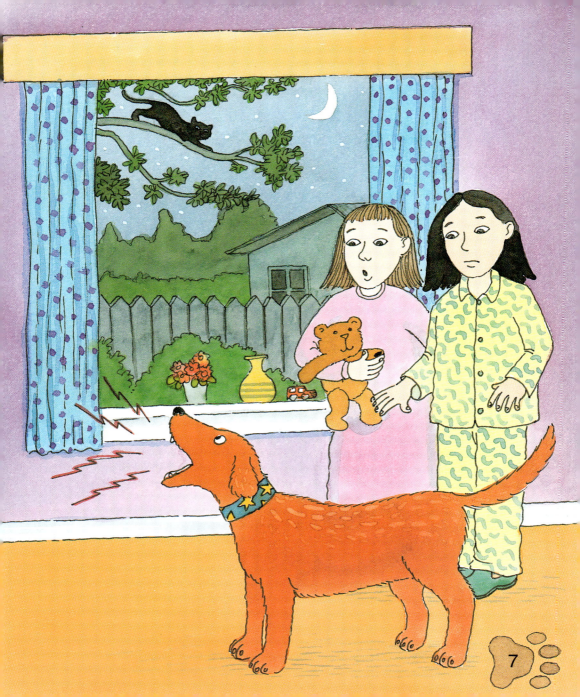

Finally, Dad says, "Stella must go to dog school!"

Now we say, "Sit!"
and Stella sits.

Now we say, "Heel!"
and Stella
walks next to us.

Now we say, "Stay!" and Stella stays.

But we say, "Quiet!" and...

...Stella still barks and barks.